THINKING THEOLOGICALLY about
Haves &
Have Nots

$$$

BROKE

(HAVE)

LOVE

NO LOVE

HAVE

LEMON

(Have not)

HAVES & HAVE-NOTS

Neal Christie

Eliezer Valentín-Castañón

Cynthia Abrams

Clayton Childers

Jeff Prothro

HAVES & HAVE-NOTS

Cover Design: Keely Moore

MANUFACTURED IN THE UNITED STATES OF AMERICA

07 08 09 10 11 12 13—10 9 8 7 6 5 4 3

Contents

Writers
Bios

Neal Christie, Eliezer Valentín-Castañón, Cynthia Abrams, Clayton Childers, and Jeff Prothro, are staff of the General Board of Church and Society of The United Methodist Church. As part of their work, they are involved with the Seminars Program, which provides youth opportunities to understand difficult social issues from a faith perspective. Neal Christie is assistant general secretary for resourcing congregational life; Eliezer Valentín-Castañón is program director for racial and restorative justice; Cynthia Abrams is program director for alcohol and other addictions and health care; Clayton Childers is program director for annual conference relations; Jeff Prothro, an intern at the board, is also a student at Wesley Theological Seminary.

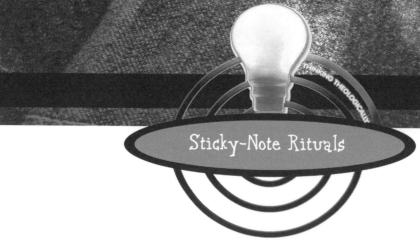

Sticky-Note Rituals

Rituals are like sticky-notes—they remind us of what's really important. We put them in prominent places so that we won't forget what we need to do each day, each hour, each minute.

That's why we begin and end session with these ritualized sayings from Scripture—to remind us of God's faithfulness and love. God's people have been saying these reminders to one another for centuries.

Opening

Leader: Steadfast love and faithfulness will meet;
Righteousness and peace will kiss each other.

Class: Faithfulness will spring up from the ground,
and righteousness will look down from the sky.

All: The Lord will give what is good and
our land will yield an increase.

—From **Psalm 85:10-12**

Closing

All: "It is God who is at work in you, enabling you both to will and to work for God's good pleasure." Amen.

—From **Philippians 2:13**

Picture the Gap

For the next few weeks, we will be studying "haves and have-nots"—a short-hand way of referring to the gap between people who have sufficient resources to meet their needs (and some of their wants) and those who do not.

- **Haves:** Individuals and groups who have ready access to the resources they need for a positive and full life

- **Have-nots:** Individuals and groups who do not have access to needed resources and who consequently suffer in a variety of ways

Based on these definitions, what do you think "resources needed for a positive and full life" would include? Give some examples.

What's the Real Problem?

The church, in response to trust in Jesus Christ as Lord, has over the past 2000 years became expert in providing for basic human needs: food, water, shelter, and love. These acts on behalf of others we call charity or mercy or compassion. They remind us of our own need for mercy in the eyes of God and our neighbors.

Acts of charity or mercy or compassion have over time become synonymous with being Christian. But our compassion toward the have-nots can also mask why there are have-nots in the first place. Soup kitchens and meal programs, while valuable, can keep us from advocating for welfare reform, living wages, and meaningful work—the things that enable people to feed themselves. Homeless shelters, while necessary, can keep us from advocating for education, recovery programs for people suffering from addiction (drugs, alcohol, gambling, and so on), affordable housing, safe and secure communities, and better healthcare coverage—things that make having a home more possible.

Despite the efforts of Christians to feed the poor and clothe the naked, things don't seem to have changed much. While the poverty rate in the United States is the lowest it has been since the 1970s, and while we enjoy the lowest unemployment rate in thirty years, according to the 2000 U.S. Census one out of six American children is poor.

The real problem in our society today is not lack of money, food, or housing but a lack of justice. If we look for solutions to homelessness, hunger, and poverty *only* in compassionate generosity, we have not dealt with the underlying problem. In addition, the people who are poor or hungry suffer the indignity of not being able to care for their own needs but having to depend on the generosity of others, which can be withheld at any time. Though some of their needs are temporarily met, many have-nots remain have-nots.

- How would you explain the differences between "mercy, charity, or compassion" and "justice"?
- How do you react to this statement: "Despite the efforts of Christians to feed the poor and clothe the naked, things don't seem to have changed much"?
- If this statement is true, should Christians stop extending charity and compassion?
- What could Christians do to bring about justice in our society?

Jesus preached the coming reign of God when he prayed, "Our father in heaven . . . . Your kingdom come. Your will be done, on earth as it is in heaven" (Matthew 6:9-10). As Christians, we too are called to pray that we might help bring about God's reign on earth.

Theo-WHAT?

Living the Christian life involves two very important questions:

- **How do we know what God thinks about an issue?**
- **How do we know what God wants us to do about that issue?**

That is the essence of theology, or "the study of God."

- *Theo:* the Greek word for *God*
- *ology*: the Greek suffix for "the study of"

In this study we will be asking these two questions about the gap between the haves and have-nots. In other words, we'll be "thinking theologically" about this issue.

theology—
the study of God

discern—
to distinguish; to have clearness of mental sight

theological framework—
a system or method for understanding God's truth. It gives shape and structure to an issue the way a frame gives shape to a house.

Thinking Theologically

Several centuries ago, an Anglican minister named John Wesley gave his people a practical way of deciding—or discerning—God's view on any given topic, including the gap between the haves and have-nots.

A careful study of Wesley's writings and sermons gives us a four-step theological framework for discerning God's perspective.

This framework helps us discover how God wants us to act. As a four-wall framework gives shape and stability to a house, Wesley's four-step framework gives us a reliable method for discerning the truth. The steps are Scripture, experience, reason, and tradition. This method is called the Wesleyan Quadrilateral.

The Wesleyan Quadrilateral

 Scripture: What the Bible Says

The Bible is God's Word for our lives, and it contains everything we need for salvation in Jesus Christ. Scripture is our primary guide for faith and practice. In it we witness God's loving intent throughout the history of God's people; through the life, death, and resurrection of Jesus; and through the Spirit-empowered history of the early church. And by it, we are shown how to be purposeful members of the kingdom of God in the here and now.

 Experience: What Experience Tells Us

Experience—the trials and joys of real life—tests and molds our Christian beliefs. It brings to life the truths revealed in Scripture. Experience is the one step that is truly your own. It gives each person's faith a unique flavor.

Reason: What Makes Sense

Reason is the ability we all have to ask questions and arrive at conclusions, using our intellect. Our minds are gifts from God. The Christian faith is a worldview held by intelligent, thinking people of all walks of life.

Tradition: What the Church Teaches

Tradition is our faith heritage: the common practices and beliefs of the Christian church throughout the centuries.

Things to Keep in Mind

Wesley believed that Scripture is the most important step in the theological process, although the other three steps are still necessary.

Why should we use all four components of the Quadrilateral when discerning the truth—not just "reason" or "experience" alone?

- If we use our reason alone, we might come to rely on all sorts of lofty theories that have never been tested.

- If we use our experience alone, we might rely too much on our own finite perspective, which is tainted by sin.

- If we use the traditions of the church alone, we might limit the work of the Holy Spirit or ignore the fact that the history of the church is also tainted with sin.

- And if we take little bits of Scripture alone, we may never know the broader biblical story or understand each passage in its historical and cultural contexts.

We must put all four components of the Quadrilateral together to get a comprehensive, Christian understanding of any topic, including the gap between the haves and have-nots.

Movie Review

Watch the movie clip. As you watch, keep in mind your assigned step from the Wesleyan Quadrilateral (one of the four below). Then use your step to respond to the message of the movie.

Experience

- What have you, or others you know, experienced that relates to the events portrayed in this scene? In other words, does this accurately represent life as you know it? Why, or why not?

- Will this scene stick in your mind for weeks to come? Why or why not? What makes the scene memorable or forgettable?

- Have you ever witnessed extreme poverty, perhaps while traveling or in your own community? If so, where and when?

- Does your experience relate to any of the issues raised by the documentary? How?

Reason

- Based on this scene, what message do you think this movie is trying to convey? What are your thoughts on that message?

- Do you agree or disagree with the director's viewpoint? How is your perspective different from the filmmakers'?

- What solutions would you offer to solve the problems or answer the questions raised by the scene? Which have already been attempted? Which alternatives need to be tried?

- Is the scene criticizing any particular group? If so, whom?

Scripture

- What values are at play in this scene? In other words, what do the filmmakers think is important?

- How are the filmmakers' values consistent or inconsistent with what Jesus says in **Matthew 5:1-11**?

- Based on your knowledge of Scripture, what is your response to the scene? What, do you think, does it have to offer Christians?

- How do you think one of the Old Testament prophets (such as Jeremiah, Isaiah, or Amos) would respond to the scene?

Tradition

- How might people in your congregation respond to the scene? (You don't need to name individuals.)

- Do you think the opinions of the filmmakers is consistent with the opinions of most members of your congregation? Why, or why not?

- Would people in your congregation affirm or reject the viewpoint being represented in the film? Why might they affirm or reject this message?

- How often is the plight of the poor in other countries prayed for or brought to light during worship? If not often, why?

Think About It!

What would the world look like if there were no longer a gap
between the rich and poor? What would the world look like if
every person had more than enough food, clothing, shelter,
work, education, healthcare, and love? Draw a picture that
somehow represents that world. Where do you fit in this picture?
Where is role of the church? Find a way to include yourself and
the church in your picture.

2

What's the Real Problem?

Scripture

Holy Scripture speaks frequently about money, wealth, and possessions. In fact, there are few subjects the Bible addresses more. Often in Scripture wealth is considered a threat to faith because of its ability to capture our hearts and lead us away from singular devotion to God. This concern is clearly evident in these warnings:

"You cannot serve both God and wealth."

—**Matthew 6:24b**

"For the love of money is a root of all kinds of evil, and in their eagerness to be rich some have wandered away from the faith and pierced themselves with many pains."

—**1 Timothy 6:10**

These teachings were given before audiences who would not have been particularly wealthy. In Jesus' day in the Near East there was a pronounced social divide between a small segment of powerful and wealthy haves and the vast majority of people, who would have been considered have-nots. The first century Roman world did not have a middle class like that of twenty-first century America. By and large Jesus' followers would have been considered have-nots because of their lack of political power, inherited or earned wealth, social standing, or formal education.

There were, however, some among Jesus followers among the haves. Luke 8:3 suggests that among Jesus' followers Joanna, Susanna, and other women were of significant financial means because of their generous support of Jesus' ministry.

Throughout his ministry Jesus consistently challenged all those who would follow him to trust entirely in God, not in the power and promise of wealth. "Do not be afraid, little flock," he said, "for it is your Father's good pleasure to give you the kingdom. Sell your possessions, and give alms. Make purses for yourselves that do not wear out, an unfailing treasure in heaven, where no thief comes near and no moth destroys. For where your treasure is, there your heart will be also" **(Luke 12:32-34).**

• When persons put their trust in something other than God, they separate themselves from God. We call that _____, which manifests itself in many ways: greed, hoarding, looking out for "number one," abuse of power, materialism, and so on.

Bible 101

From the **Law:** Read **Deuteronomy 24:17-22.**

Very early in their life as a people the Hebrews were instructed to care for the alien, the orphan, and the widow.

• Why were these three classes of people singled out?
• Why are God's words in verse 22—"Remember that you were a slave in the land of Egypt"—a crucial part of the Law for the Hebrews?

From the **Prophets:** Read aloud **Amos 8:4-7.**

A key measure of Israel's distance from God was how it treated the poor. As the prophets called Israel back to God, they boldly confronted these injustices.

• Why would how a nation or people treats the poor be a measure of faithfulness to God?

From **John the Baptist:** Read aloud **Luke 3:7-14.**

In this passage John challenges those who have come out into the wilderness to hear his preaching to return to God from the evil ways that dominate their lives. They are overcome by John's challenging message. They know that they are not right with God, and they plead for guidance—specific guidance—about what they must do to restore their relationships with God.

- What do John's three instructions (to the crowd, the tax collectors, the soldiers) all have in common?

From **Jesus:** Read aloud **Luke 4:16-21.**

Jesus' first sermon outlines his mission. Each of these four categories of people he came to help—the poor, the captives, the blind, and the oppressed—is symbolic of a larger grouping.

- Who do you think today would be included under each of these headings: persons who are poor, captive, blind, oppressed?
- Why do you think Jesus focused on these particular people in the very first sermon he ever preached?
- How did Jesus live out this promise to lift of up the poor, the imprisoned, the blind and the oppressed? What particular stories or parables demonstrate his concern for these peoples?

OPTIONAL DISCUSSION: At the end of his reading Jesus states that he has come to "proclaim the year of the Lord's favor" (verse 19). Many scholars believe this is a reference to the Year of Jubilee (see **Leviticus 25:8-55**). In this Scripture God instructs God's people to celebrate every fiftieth year as the Year of Jubilee. During the Year of Jubilee the Israelites were to:

1) Forgive all debts that had accumulated,
2) Release their slaves, and
3) Return to its original owners all land that had been sold away by people who found themselves in financial difficulty.

Jubilee was intended to be a year of liberation for the poor, the enslaved, and the oppressed.

- How would such a Year of Jubilee help decrease the gap between the haves and the have-nots?
- Though most people do not celebrate the Jubilee Year exactly as it is described in Leviticus, what do people today do to carry out God's intentions for the Jubilee Year?

From the **Early Church**: Read aloud **Acts 2:43-47**.

The early Christians took to heart Christ's call to love one another. They were so touched by the Spirit of God that they begin to care for one another the same way family members might do so. The group as a whole shared their property and were united to help all among them who were in need. No one went without. No one was privileged above anyone else.

• What does this Scripture tell us about the way the early church addressed the needs of the have-nots? Who took responsibility?
• How does this approach to meeting the needs of others preserve people's dignity?
• In what ways does your church act in this spirit?

OPTIONAL DISCUSSION: Some scholars suggest that this passage is an idealized remembrance of "the good old days" and that if such a period of church history did exist, it did not last very long.

• If that is so, why do you think this idea of shared property and resources would not have lasted? How might this way of living together be difficult to maintain?

Just Imagine

Read **1 Corinthians 12:12-26**. Then make a list of at least ten low-paying jobs you can think of.

1.   6.

2.   7.

3.   8.

4.   9.

5.   10.

- What if all the people who work low-wage jobs did not show up for work tomorrow? How would life be different if no one did these jobs?

Gordon Chamberlain has written in his book *Upon Whom We Depend* that there is a large class of people in the United States—a poverty class—who do a vast variety of jobs necessary for our society. But because they are paid so little for their work, they do not have enough money to live their lives in dignity. Their salaries are insufficient to cover the cost of housing, utilities, transportation, insurance, childcare, healthcare, food, and daily necessities. Often they work two, sometimes three, jobs trying to meet their financial needs.

Inevitably, they run up debts on credit cards, beg from family and friends, skip meals, risk having their children go unsupervised, do without healthcare, drive uninsured and unreliable cars. They often end up homeless and on the street. At times they are able to acquire emergency assistance from hospitals, churches, charity agencies, or the government but they are trapped by a poverty system that has created a poverty cycle from which many of them are never able to escape.

Chamberlain suggests that most Americans believe the working poor are dependent on us; but in actuality, we as a society are dependent on them. Every day, they do a vast number of menial jobs that allow us to enjoy the comfortable life. Who would clean the buildings, pick up the trash, unload the trucks, answer the phones, care for the children, cook the food, pick the fruit, or run the machines if no one was willing to work for low wages? Yet, every day many people doing these and other essential jobs are not able to get through the month without depending on help from friends, charities, or government assistance.

- How does **1 Corinthians 12:12-26** relate to Dr. Chamberlain's point?
- Read verse 26 again. How does our society suffer by having members who are living in poverty?

19

Think About It!

- Would you prefer to be dependent upon someone else's being willing to give you what you need (food, clothing, housing, and so forth) or to be able to acquire those things through your own ability?

As Christians, we are called to be compassionate—to help those who are in need. However, we are also called to work for justice—to look for long-term solutions that will change the systems responsible for poverty and make it possible for all people to have adequate means for a life of dignity.

- Of everything you have learned today what has had the greatest impact on your thinking?

- Which Scripture verse that you read today was the most memorable or meaningful? Why?

The Poverty Cycle Drama

This drama requires three volunteers. To begin, Volunteer 1 will have two coats and one can of food; Volunteer 2 will have two cans of food and one coat; and Volunteer 3 will have nothing.

Volunteer 3 (V3): Cries and holds arms and shivers as if in extreme cold

Volunteer 1: Takes pity on V3 and gives up one coat to help

Volunteer 3: Looks satisfied with warmth—but only for a moment—then grabs stomach and acts as though he or she will die unless he or she has something to eat

Volunteer 2: Motions to V3 to signal that he or she will give V3 a can of food if V3 will give him or her the coat

Volunteer 3: Agrees to take the can and give up the coat, joyfully eats the food and looks satisfied—but only for a moment—then begins to shiver in the cold again

Volunteer 2: Eventually gives in and gives V3 one coat

Volunteer 3: Looks satisfied with warmth—but only for a moment—then grabs stomach and acts as though he or she will die unless he or she has something to eat

Volunteer 1: Motions to V3 that he or she will give V3 a can of food if V3 will give him or her the coat

Volunteer 3: Agrees to take the can and give up the coat, joyfully eats the food and looks satisfied—but only for a moment—then begins to shiver in the cold again

21

Experience

Power and Privilege

In the left-hand column are descriptions of groups of people in US society who have a greater degree of power and privilege than others. In the space to the right, make notes detailing more specifically who those persons are and why they have power and privilege.

What

- people who have unearned or inherited privileges or power simply because of their

  age
  race
  gender
  religion
  nationality
  economic status
  physical or mental ability
  family they were born into

- people who can vote
- people who can read
- people who can live where they want to live
- people without physical or mental challenges
- people who are educated

Who and Why

Power: the ability to act effectively; legitimate access to resources; the official capacity to exercise control or influence over others

Privilege: a special advantage, immunity, or right held because of rank or status; often used to the exclusion or detriment of others

"Washing one's hands of the conflict between the powerful and the powerless means to side with he powerful, not to be neutral." —Paulo Friere

What's the Real Problem?

Since the late 1960's, profits in the United States have actually spiraled downward. One effective way for an economic system comprised of haves and have-nots to restore profits is to get workers to work harder, longer, and for less pay. Over the last few decades, gutting welfare support to poor children and families, moving factories abroad, and replacing factory jobs with low-wage service jobs have all been used to increase profit for a few at the expense of many.

This drive to increase profits for the few has amounted to a fundamental restructuring of the United States economy and has had horrendous consequences. Homelessness has spread across the nation. Poverty rates and unemployment have skyrocketed. Phrases like the "working poor" and "discouraged workers" have became part of our everyday vocabulary.

These policies have contributed to the creation of a permanently unemployed "underclass" of poor people, which is made up predominantly of people of color.

- Why might this resulting underclass of poor people be made up predominantly of people of color?

- How does this information about the real problem relate to your understanding of power and privilege?

Who Has the Money?

- Suppose you had $100 to divide among 100 people. What would be fair way to distribute the money?

If you were to divide that $100 based on the distribution of wealth in the United States, here's who gets the money:

- 1 person gets $38.10 each
- 4 people get $5.32 each
- 5 people get $2.30 each
- 10 people get $1.25 each
- 20 people get .60 each
- 20 people get .23 each
- 40 people get half of a penny each

Do the Math!

- How many times more money does the wealthiest person make than the 40 poorest persons make combined?

- Who makes more total money, the wealthiest 5 persons or the other 95 persons?

(Because the decimals have been rounded, these numbers will not add up to exactly $100.)

24

Rotten Apples

After World War II, the United States entered what is often called the Golden Age of Capitalism (1950–1973). During this period white women were encouraged to stay in the home, white men could be the sole breadwinners, and suburbs sprang up across the United States. And while real wages increased and racial inequality began to decrease during this period in American history, it was also during this time that the gap between the rich and poor began to widen significantly.

As the gap has grown, the numbers of people living in prisons and ghettos has also increased. The prison population grew from 200,000 in 1970 to 2,000,000 in 2000. Why?

- The purpose of prisons is to remove the "rotten apples" from society for the good of everyone else. Are there really ten times as many "rotten apples" today as there were thirty years ago? What do you think?

- Why would a gap between haves and have-nots contribute to an exploding prison population?

One possible explanation is that prisons are functioning to control the impoverished—the "collateral damage" of an economic system that has created a distinct group of haves at the expense of the have-nots.

Some people believe that a rising tide lifts all boats (in a growing economy everyone becomes better off than they were). But this theory does not always prove true. In the last thirty years the growing U.S. economy has lifted some boats more than others. Too many people are "left in the sand." Many of these people are sitting in prison.

"The test of the sincerity of one's prayer is the willingness to labor on its behalf." —St. John Chrysostom

Think About It!

• Of everything you have learned and experienced today, what has had the greatest impact on your thinking?

• What have you learned today that you didn't know before?

• How does this knowledge affect the way you think about the gap between haves and have-nots?

• How might you interact differently with persons who are poor as a result of what you have learned? with persons who are rich?

"We have grasped the mystery of the atom and rejected the Sermon on the Mount. Ours is a world of nuclear giants and ethical infants. We know more about war than we do about peace, more about killing than we do about living, more about acquiring than we do sharing." —General Omar Bradley

4

Tradition

Needs Vs. Wants

Have you ever gone shopping for one specific item and come home with a bunch of other things too? With all the neat stuff and all the persuasive ads, it's so easy to *want* things. But do we *need* them?

On *Clean Sweep,* a television show on The Learning Channel, a team goes to a home that is drowning in stuff. They work on two rooms, initially pulling everything outside to be sorted—to throw away, sell at a yard sale or donate, or keep. The resulting piles tell the tale of how easy it is to acquire more than is needed. Does anyone really *need* eighteen pairs of shoes?

Do a mental "clean sweep" of your room. What don't you *need*? Make a list of at least seven things in each of these categories:

Throw Away	Sell or Donate
1.	1.
2.	2.
3.	3.
4.	4.
5.	5.
6.	6.
7.	7.

"Do I need this or do I just want it?"

As a Christian, ask yourself this question before you buy something. Decide in light of God's bigger picture.

27

What's the Real Problem?

Some people would say that justice is impossible in our time because there are simply not enough resources present in our world for all to flourish. But in fact, God has created a world of tremendous abundance, a world that provides sufficient means for all people to live full and meaningful lives. Indeed, Scripture states that Jesus came that all might "have life, and have it abundantly (**John 10:10**). This vision is not an empty promise. It is a real possibility.

However, when we consider our world's resources, one thing is clear: Over the long term, sustaining the current lifestyle and energy consumption of people in the most developed nations is impossible. The haves cannot continue to consume the world's resources at their current rate, or the resources will be depleted, affecting everyone.

Flourish—to do well, to thrive

Sustainable—able to be maintained or kept going

Does stopping this over-consumption mean that the world's privileged and wealthy must now be asked to suffer so that the world's poor can be uplifted? No. God does not desire that any should suffer. God has given us resources sufficient for all the world's people to flourish and live lives of dignity. Abundant life for all, however, will require personal and systemic change. Current consumption levels by the haves are unsustainable. Our world is simply out of balance.

But many who are currently privileged may find that they flourish more by having and doing less. Too many possessions can keep us from flourishing as whole persons. As Jesus reminds us:

"Take care! Be on your guard against all kinds of greed; for one's life does not consist in the abundance of possessions"

—**Luke 12:15**

For many a simpler life is a happier life. People who have intentionally chosen to simplify their lives often claim that their simplified ways of living are much more fulfilling than their previous lifestyles.

• How could having too much stuff get in the way of an abundant life? (Think of the *Clean Sweep* experience, as one example.)

• What kind of personal change could the haves make in order to assure a sustainable lifestyle for themselves *and* the have-nots?

• How does this information relate to the discussion from Needs Vs. Wants (page 27)?

The Church at Work

The problems of poverty, including hunger, homelessness, and healthcare, are huge and complex. What can one person do?

Even if one person can do very little, the good news is that one person joined with another person and another person and on and on can make an enormous difference. Working together is one of the strengths of the church. The church unites people to address more effectively the big problems.

Boycott for Change

At this writing, The United Methodist Church, the Presbyterian Church (USA), the United Church of Christ, the Christian Church (Disciples of Christ), and other Christian denominations through the National Council of Churches are urging members to refuse to eat at Taco Bell. This fast-food chain purchases many of its tomatoes from a supplier that pays the laborers who pick tomatoes only $7,500 a year—well below the poverty line! These wages have not increased for over twenty-five years. If Taco Bell were to pay just one cent more per pound of tomatoes (about 1/4 of a cent per chalupa), the workers' income would double! In addition to meager wages, most of the laborers have no health insurance.

The church sees this injustice and is calling for action. The fact that you, your friends, and other Christians refuse to eat at the popular restaurant until the wrong is righted puts pressure on Taco Bell, its suppliers, and its parent company (Yum, Incorporated) to change. Yum, Incorporated is the world's largest restaurant corporation, so it has power to effect serious change.

- What's the "baby in the river"?
- What's happening "upstream"?

Reduce Hunger

Hunger is a global issue. In many countries of Africa and Asia, 80–90 percent of the people are hungry. In Latin America, the figure is 50 percent. Occasionally, the news media will show pictures of starving children with their bony arms and legs and distended bellies. These few pictures represent the millions of others crushed by famine and unequal distribution of food.

While starvation is less frequent in the United States, "food insecurity" is prevalent. Significant numbers of people do not know where their next meal will come from. Inadequate food and poor nutrition lead to poor health and learning problems. Among those most likely to be food insecure in the United States are racial- and ethnic-minority families headed by single women, children, the elderly, and groups in regions such as Appalachia and near the Southwest border. The church steps in with feeding programs but also with political clout, working within systems and policies to make changes. With regard to hunger the church is committed to both acts of mercy and acts of justice!

- What's the "baby in the river"?
- What's happening "upstream"?

Tackle Community Needs

In some communities church leaders of several denominations have organized into larger groups to effect change in their communities. These groups research their communities' needs then work through the political process to ensure that all voices are heard and responded to. Such community organizations have advocated successfully for better public transportation (a necessity for many working poor people), for building more housing that lower income families can afford, and so on. Being organized and vocal gets the attention of policy makers.

- What's the "baby in the river"?
- What's happening "upstream"?

His Ministry

John Wesley, an eighteenth century clergyman, founded the Methodist Movement, which rapidly spread from England to America. Today, churches that claim Wesleyan roots have more than ten million members throughout the world. Part of what spurred the movement forward was Wesley's and other leaders' commitment to justice on behalf of the have-nots.

When Wesley was ordained, he took **Luke 4:16-21** as the text of his first sermon—Jesus' own call in life to liberate those oppressed by sickness and poverty who would otherwise be destined to live as society's have-nots. For Wesley economic issues were not just abstract ideas related to business and finance; he believed that dealing with economic justice in light of Scripture was part of what it meant to be a disciple of Christ.

In his "Sermon on the Good Steward," Wesley highlighted our obligation to God for managing faithfully the resources that God has placed in our hands. In his "Sermon on the Use of Money," he helped believers understand the importance of using well the great resource, called money, that God has placed in our hands. His point was that our money belongs to God and that true disciples of Jesus Christ cannot misuse this resource without putting their relationship with God at risk.

In his ministry Wesley clearly took the side of the poor and the oppressed in eighteenth-century England. Wesley and the Methodist societies were committed to ministry with the have-nots. Methodists then and Methodists since have had a positive impact on economic conditions in their communities and nations and around the world as they have advocated and worked for justice.

His Life

However, Wesley was not only an skilled leader; he also inspired and witnessed to others through his own practices of faith. Not content simply to preach about being a good steward, he learned frugality in his spending and use of possessions from his early days as a financially-strapped college student at Oxford University.

At Lincoln College (part of Oxford), Wesley learned to live on a maximum of 28 English pounds a year. In subsequent years, Wesley's income rose, but he continued to live on the 28 pounds he lived on as a student; he gave away the rest of his money. Over time, he resorted to simply "saving" (being thrifty in all the ways he could) and then "giving" away all that he could give.

In his later years, Wesley generated much income from his written publications—as much a thousand pounds profit each year. Wesley was surprised to find that he had "unawares become rich." In his lifetime Wesley is said to have disposed of over 30,000 pounds (Sermon #87, "The Danger of Riches").

Today and My Life

Christian financial counselors today challenge people to live below their means, to not go into debt, but to choose wisely what they buy (remember Needs Vs. Wants—page 27), and to plan for purchases. With this kind of attention to taking care of their money, people are actually more free to do what is truly important to them, and they are in a position to help others.

• How can you take the example and teachings of John Wesley and today's Christian financial counselors and apply them to your life?

> "Live simply so that others may simply live."
> —Anonymous

Think About It!

- Of everything you have learned and experienced today, what has had the greatest impact on your thinking?

- What have you learned today that you didn't know before?

- Would you classify the purchases you have made in the past week more as needs or as wants?

- What, of all that you *have*, are you willing to commit to help those who *have not*?

"It is a fundamental principle with us that to renounce reason is to renounce religion, that religion and reason go hand in hand, and that all irrational religion is false religion."

—John Wesley

5

Reason

Puzzling it Out

Reason is the God-given ability to use our minds to ask questions and to reach conclusions. It allows us to analyze problems and create solutions instead of simply accepting things as they are. Reason allows you, as a person of faith, to detect when situations and values are out of sync with God's values. When this happens, we can work together with God to come up with solutions.

What's the Real Problem?

Evidence shows that there is an adequate supply of food in the world today; no one should go hungry. Food is simply not made available to everyone. Inequitable distribution has created the problem. Some people have more than enough; others do not have enough.

Likewise, with creativity and commitment, adequate housing could be provided for all the world's people. Working together we could create new systems that enable the poor of the world to buy or construct dwellings that are warm, dry, and of adequate size. Doing so is simply a matter of priorities.

Many nations in our world have made great strides toward creating healthcare systems that provide care for all of their citizens without regard to employment or financial status. More steps must be taken to insure that healthcare is universally available in countries where many people still do not have access.

Profound change is possible only if the world's people would make adequate food, housing, and healthcare a global priority.

The evidence is already established:

⌘ Over the last few decades nations, the United Nations, and non-governmental organizations have come together to cut world hunger rates dramatically.

⌘ At the turn of the new millennium a number of the world's wealthiest nations stepped forward to significantly cut the suffocating debt owed by many of the world poorest nations (though much more still needs to be done).

⌘ Most recently, commitments were made by developed nations, through the Millennial Challenge Account, to make available billions of dollars every year to help the world's poor have greater access to medical care, especially to AIDS medications.

Progress is possible. Poverty can be overcome. The problem is one of inequitable distribution and lack of political will.

• What does the term "political will" mean to you?

• What can individuals and groups do to have an impact on the political will of their leaders?

Case Study 1: Poverty and the Casino

An American Indian tribe that lives on a reservation near your town wants to build a big casino that would be located very near your school. Some store owners in town are very happy about this proposed development because it could potentially bring extra business to their stores.

Many locals, however, are unhappy about the prospect of a nearby casino. Your pastor even preached against gambling last Sunday. Most people say the casino will ruin the town by bringing in heavy traffic, crime, and addiction. Some people have even formed a protest group.

A town council meeting is called to air concerns about the casino. There is a lot of name-calling and even some racist remarks made at the meeting.

You have noticed that the American Indian students who are in your classes at school often do not wear nice new clothes or popular brand sneakers. You often drive by or through parts of the reservation and notice that many of the houses are small and in disrepair.

Most people in your town just ignore living conditions on the reservation, but you wonder about what you have seen. American Indian tribal leaders come to the town meeting and say they just want to help their tribe get out of poverty.

- Since the church is opposed to gambling, how can this disparity in wealth be solved without building a casino?

- What would be the best thing to happen to the American Indian tribe if the casino were built? The worst?

- Who should ultimately decide whether the casino is built?

Case Study 2: Unequal Valedictorians

When Sam graduated at the top of his class, he had earned 20 hours of college credit from Advanced Placement courses and had gained valuable experience with the debate team and the jazz band. He was easily admitted to Harvard.

Two hundred miles away in the same state, Sue also graduated at the top of her class, but she was not able to take trigonometry (let alone calculus), physics, music, or art. She had no Advanced Placement courses available to her. She was admitted to a small state school with a requirement that she take remedial courses.

Is Sue not as smart as Sam? No, these teenagers' educations have been affected by where they live. Sam lives in a wealthy county, where the average income is $70,000; Sue lives in a rural county with an average income of $20,000.

Sue's county does not have the tax base (businesses, sales, and property taxes) that Sam's county has. Since schools rely on these taxes to operate, the schools are doomed to inequity. Or are they?

- Is being a have or a have-not just based on factors as simple as where one lives? what color one's skin is? who one's family is?

- What responsibility do the people in Sam's county have for the people in Sue's county? Any? What's the role of the state?

- What can Christians do to assure more equal opportunities for young persons to have a good education?

"Be a part of the solution, not the problem"

—Anonymous

Youth Making a Difference

How do people make a difference in the face of problems that are big and complex? How can young persons make a difference?

⌘ "Why can kids buy a gun right in the neighborhood in a few hours but have to take a bus outside of the neighborhood to buy school supplies?" asked Sherman Spears with Teens on Target at a press conference in Oakland, California. This testimony helped the city council pass a gun control ordinance in a community divided into haves and have-nots.

⌘ Peer educators in Buffalo, New York, learned of a proposal considered by the state legislature to reduce funding for comprehensive health education. One high school student made the statement: "My friends and classmates are dying from alcohol, drugs, and AIDS and poverty. The proposed cut for school health would mean only five cents per student. That's the price of a stick of gum, Is that all we are worth?" The state legislature changed its policy.

⌘ Seventh graders in the urban areas of Dallas, Texas, and Washington, D.C. with the help of their churches surveyed their neighborhood block by block. They decided one problem they wanted to tackle was the number of liquor stores near their schools and church. They videotaped their own communities then examined the suburbs. They found very few liquor stores in the suburbs—and none near schools. Students met with the zoning commission and held press conferences in front of liquor stores to call attention to the problem.

Real advocacy comes from grassroots people lobbying or advocating for what they believe is right.

Working Together

Work together to create a list of 10 things people—including youth—can do to bridge the gap between haves and have-nots. Circle one or two that you will commit to.

1.

2.

3.

4.

5.

6.

7.

8.

9.

10.

Where to Go to Help

For more information on groups supporting the have-nots, look at these websites:

Project South: Institute for the Elimination of Poverty and Genocide: *www.projectsouth.org*

Heifer Project International: *www.heifer.org*. This organization provides animals and education to help persons around the world with adequate nutrition and an increased economic base.

The General Board of Church and Society, The United Methodist Church: *www.umc-gbcs.org*

The General Board of Global Missions, The United Methodist Church: *www.gbgm-umc.org*

Habitat for Humanity International: *www.habitat.org*. This organization focuses on providing affordable housing.

Society of St. Andrew: *www.endhunger.org*. This organization uses the biblical practice of gleaning to salvage usable food and see that it is distributed. The Potato Project and the Potato Drop are two of their programs. The organization also provides hunger education and includes youth in their work projects.

Social Principles of The United Methodist Church: *www.umc.org/interior.asp?mid=1686*

UMPower is a free and easy way to make your voice known to Congress and elected officials in your state or hometown and to send your opinions to newspapers in your area. Check it out at *www.capwiz.com/gbcs/home*. Also, contact the General Board of Church and Society for youth empowerment training and opportunities to organize around poverty and related issues: 202-488-5600.

Relieving debt makes a world of difference to people and developing nations who have more than paid back what they have owed. Learn more through **Jubilee USA** and ask for their video *Cancel the Debt, Now!*, *www.jubileeusa.org*, 202-783-3566 and the **National Labor Committee** for videos on how to stop child labor and sweatshop labor, 212-242-0700.

Organize a letter writing campaign to your members of Congress and learn more about the acute and effect of hunger from **Bread for the World:** *www.bfw.org*.

Check out the **Youth Action Line** for dozens of ideas for pursuing youth led campaigns for social change. Resource Central offers links to 250 other sites, leads of grant monies, free advise for your projects, plus media outlets: *www.youthactivism.com*.

To host a panel of speakers and participate in a public campaign to end hunger and homelessness contact Habitat for Humanity (*www.habitat.org*), **National Coalition for the Homeless** (*www.nationalhomeless.org*), or **National Student Campaign Against Hunger and Homelessness** (*www.pirg.org/nscahh*).

"**Co/Motion Guide to Youth-Led Social Change**" is a reader friendly manual packed with inspiration and strategies to help young people effect change in their communities. Order it from the **Alliance for Justice:** 202-822-6070, *www.afj.org*.

Think About It!

- Of everything you have learned and experienced today, what has had the greatest impact on your thinking?

- What have you learned today that you didn't know before?

- How does this knowledge affect the way you think about the haves and have-nots?

- How might you interact differently with persons who are among the haves? among the have-nots?

- What ideas do you have for becoming "part of the solution"?

Quiz Time

Thinking Theologically As a personal challenge, answer the following questions as best you can:

1. What are the four components of the Wesleyan Quadrilateral?

2. Why is it important that we use all four components of the Quadrilateral in discerning God's truth, not just one or two?

3. List two Scripture passages that were a part of this study that are important to you in relating to the issue of the gap between the haves and have-nots. What guidance do they give you?

4. What was the main activity you did for Session Three (Experience)? What did you learn from this activity that surprised you?

5. What did you learn from church tradition or from individual Christians that gives you hope that this problem will ultimately be resolved? How do these examples inspire you?

6. As you examine this issue of the disparity between haves and have-nots, what does your intellect, or reasoning, tell you?

7. Name one thing that you learned from this study that you'll never forget.

What's the Real Problem?

☒ **Sin** and its manifestations: greed, hoarding, looking out for number one, and so forth (page 8)

☒ **Lack of justice** (pages 15–16)

☒ **Restructuring of the economy** (page 24)

☒ **Unsustainable lifestyle** (pages 28–29)

☒ **Political will** (pages 35–36)

Each of these has been put forward as the real problem behind the gap between the haves and have-nots. Which of these do you think is the biggest factor driving the disparity between the rich and poor?

For your round table discussion:

1) Read over the material related to your assigned point of view.

2) Underline or highlight in your book important points that you wish to bring to the discussion.

3) Prepare an opening statement about how your point of view is the "real problem."

4) Think of supporting evidence and examples to make your point more convincing.

Going to God in Worship

Call to Worship (from **Psalm 85:10-12**)

Leader: Steadfast love and faithfulness will meet;
Righteousness and peace will kiss each other;

Class: Faithfulness will spring up from the ground,
and righteousness will look down from the sky.

All: The Lord will give what is good,
and our land will yield an increase.

Opening prayer:

Leader: Most gracious and loving God, we gather in your name
to faithfully live out your call.

Class: We seek justice for the poor.
We seek love for the needy.
We seek guidance for the wealthy.
You give hope to all.

All: Your love surrounds all creation, demanding equality
in Your Holy Name. Amen.

Praise Songs

Scripture Readings:

- **Deuteronomy 15:7-11**
- **Matthew 5:3-11**
- **Acts 4:32-35**
- **James 5:1-6**

Prayers of Confession and Thanksgiving:

On a note card or piece of paper write down both a concern and a joy that you have related to the topic of haves and have-nots. Spend a moment in silence followed with a silent prayer.

Hymn: "Jesu, Jesu"

Offering

Place your note card in the offering plate. Sing praises to God and end with prayer, noting the offering the community is giving to God, filled with joys and concerns.

Community Moments (instead of a Sermon)

Students offer reflections on what they have learned from the study.

Celebrate Holy Communion

God invites all to come to the Table.

Time of Dedication

During this time, you will be invited to participate in laying-on of hands for each participant as a way of supporting one another.

The pastor or leader will pray:

> God of all, we consecrate this your servant, (*name*). Empower (*her or him*) by your Holy Spirit to live justly and to work for justice so that all may live as you have intended—with enough. In the name of the Creator, the Son, and the Holy Spirit. Amen.

Benediction (You may use the Benediction on page 6.)

- If you had to state the key learnings of this entire study in one sentence, what would you say?

- What do *you* think is the real problem that causes the disparity between the haves and have-nots?

- As a result of this study, how will you change the way you interact with the have-nots? with the haves?

- Name one thing you want to change about yourself, your church, or your society as a result of this study.

- How are you going to faithfully live out God's call regarding the haves and have-nots?